Leisure & Community Services

THE
TWELVE DAYS OF
CHRISTMAS

THE
TWELVE DAYS OF CHRISTMAS

Justin Todd

LONDON
VICTOR GOLLANCZ LTD
1989

First published in Great Britain 1989
by Victor Gollancz Ltd
14 Henrietta Street, London WC2E 8QJ

Illustrations © Justin Todd 1989

British Library Cataloguing in Publication Data
The twelve days of Christmas
I. Title   II. Todd, Justin
823'.914[J]

ISBN 0-575-04432-2

Printed in Hong Kong by Imago Publishing Ltd

For Max and Leah

ON THE FIRST DAY OF CHRISTMAS,
My true love sent to me
A partridge in a pear tree.

On the second day of christmas,
My true love sent to me
Two turtle doves, and
A partridge in a pear tree.

On THE THIRD DAY OF CHRISTMAS,
My true love sent to me
Three French hens,
Two turtle doves, and
A partridge in a pear tree.

On the eighth day of Christmas,
My true love sent to me
Eight maids a-milking,
Seven swans a-swimming,
Six geese a-laying,
Five gold rings,
Four colly birds,
Three French hens,
Two turtle doves, and
A partridge in a pear tree.